Original title:
A Christmas Filled with Love

Copyright © 2024 Creative Arts Management OÜ
All rights reserved.

Author: Dexter Sullivan
ISBN HARDBACK: 978-9916-94-058-7
ISBN PAPERBACK: 978-9916-94-059-4

Gathering of Souls

In the kitchen, chaos reigns,
Uncle Joe has lost his brains.
The turkey's dancing on the floor,
While Grandma shouts, 'We need more!'

Cousins spill the punch again,
The dog is in a doughnut den.
Batter stains on every face,
Who knew cooking was a race?

Festive Laughter Echoing

The ornaments hang by a thread,
While Dad pretends he's well-bred.
He sticks a hat on the tree's top,
But the poor thing has lost the plot.

A snowman made of dirty socks,
A reindeer fashioned from old clocks.
Each gift wrapped with tape and glue,
Now looks like a monster, who knew?

Threads of Affection

The cat's wrapped up in ribbons bright,
While kids are plotting a pillow fight.
Aunt Sue's knitting just breaks the seams,
A sweater woven from shattered dreams.

We share our jokes, the cheese balls roll,
And laughter seems to fill the whole.
With every giggle and each cheer,
We count our blessings, year by year.

Festive Laughter Echoing

The ornaments hang by a thread,
While Dad pretends he's well-bred.
He sticks a hat on the tree's top,
But the poor thing has lost the plot.

A snowman made of dirty socks,
A reindeer fashioned from old clocks.
Each gift wrapped with tape and glue,
Now looks like a monster, who knew?

Threads of Affection

The cat's wrapped up in ribbons bright,
While kids are plotting a pillow fight.
Aunt Sue's knitting just breaks the seams,
A sweater woven from shattered dreams.

We share our jokes, the cheese balls roll,
And laughter seems to fill the whole.
With every giggle and each cheer,
We count our blessings, year by year.

Kisses Beneath the Snow

Under mistletoe, laughter grows,
A kiss on cheeks with chilly toes.
Mom slipped on ice, a scene divine,
While Dad's just happy with his wine.

We're bundled up like giant bears,
As snowflakes dance without a care.
A snowball fight turns into glee,
With hugs and laughter, just us three.

Kindred Spirits Dance in the Glow

Twinkling lights on the tree,\nWe prance like elves with glee.\nA secret stash of cookies near,\nLet's not let anyone interfere!\n\nFrosty noses, cheeks aglow,\nSliding down the hills like pros.\nHot cocoa spills, oh what a mess,\nYet laughter is our true success!

Laughter Echoes through the Snowy Streets

Snowmen sporting hats askew,\nA carrot-nosed brigade we drew.\nWith snowball fights and hasty throws,\nWe giggle at our chilly woes.\n\nMittens lost and scarves untied,\nWe tumble over, side by side.\nEvery laughter echoes clear,\nSpreading warmth, keeping cheer!

The Language of Love in Every Ornament

Bedecked in tinsel and bright beads,\nEach bauble tells of joyful deeds.\nA wobbly star, a crooked bow,\nOur love shines through the silly show.\n\nGingerbread houses, slightly lopsided,\nWe eat our failures, oh how we snided!\nIn every giggle, a story spilled,\nIn our jumbled hearts, laughter is filled!

Beneath the Stars, We Are Whole

The night sky twinkles with pure delight,\nWhile we bumble in our holiday fight.\nWith each misstep, we find our way,\nUnder the stars, we choose to stay.\n\nDancing shadows in the moonlight's gleam,\nSwirling 'round like a silly dream.\nIn every chuckle, we find our place,\nBeneath the stars, we embrace our grace!

Love Letters in the Snow

Snowflakes fall like love notes,
Stuck on hats and big red coats.
I sent my heart on a sled, you see,
But it got lost under the Christmas tree.

My snowman wears my heartfelt plea,
With carrot nose and eyes so free.
But when it rains, oh dear, oh no!
My love's dripped down—where did it go?

Embracing Winter's Glow

We dance on ice, what a sight,
Spinning and falling, what pure delight.
With every slip, laughter rings,
Who knew winter had such funny things?

Hot cocoa spills as I take a sip,
My marshmallow boat gave a funny flip.
We warm our hands by the frosty lights,
And giggle at our silly winter sights.

The Warmth of Family

With family close, the chaos begins,
Finding lost socks and matching twin pins.
Grandma's cooking with a dash of love,
But that fruitcake? It's a gift from above!

Uncle Joe sings off-key, what a sound,
While the cat's stealing turkey, look around!
We laugh till we cry, what a wild ride,
Those quirky moments make us filled with pride.

Hushed Moments by the Fire

By the fire, we gather near,
Telling stories that bring good cheer.
My dad's a joker, a laugh-a-minute,
Who knew the dog would claim the whole limit?

The flames dance and crackle, quite a show,
As Dad's sock puppet steals the fire's glow.
A pillow fight breaks, fluff fills the air,
These quiet moments, oh joy, they're rare!

Kindred Spirits United

Amidst the lights, we get so jolly,
With Santa hats that look quite folly.
We drink hot cocoa, spill it on our shoes,
While telling tales of our goofy crews.

Snowmen grin with carrots for their nose,
They wobble and jiggle, just like our toes.
We sing off-key, yet we feel so grand,
And dance like penguins, hand in hand.

Gifts of the Heart

I wrapped a gift, or so I thought,
But inside was nothing, just a silly plot.
My cat decided it was his new toy,
Now he's the happiest feline with pure joy.

Uncle Joe opened socks, two left and no right,
He laughed so hard, he nearly took flight.
We trade our blunders, laughter we send,
In the chaos of love, there are no ends.

Nuances of an Icy Night

The stars above twinkle with delight,
While we slip on ice, what a funny sight!
Hot chocolate spills from a cup on my knee,
I laugh louder because it's just me.

Prancing through snow, we trip on a mound,
Each tumble we take, we dance on the ground.
A snowball flies past, a hit gets the grin,
Not sure if it's chilly or warmth that we win.

Cradled by Kindness

Grandma's cookies have a strange little taste,
Like a secret ingredient, a sweet little waste.
Her stories are wild, and they make us snort,
As we gather around, laughter we court.

The tree is bulging with ornaments bright,
We marvel at its awkward, lopsided height.
Fuzzy socks with reindeer bring endless cheer,
For in each silly moment, love's always near.

The Gift of Presence in Every Moment

In cozy socks we gather, oh what a sight,
With mugs of cocoa, our giggles take flight.
Who spilled the sprinkles, it's all on the floor!
But laughter's the gift that we all can explore.

Each moment is precious, like cookies in jars,
We share silly stories, and dance under stars.
Unwrap the joy, it's a messy affair,
But love's in the chaos, and we all have our share.

Memories Wrapped in Ribbons of Joy

Grandma's old tales with a wink and a grin,
Wrapped up in laughter, let the stories begin.
She trips on the carpet, oh what a delight,
We can't stop our chuckles, it's pure holiday light.

As tinsel goes flying, and cats start to pounce,
We hold our bellies, just trying to bounce.
Each memory's precious, like gifts piled so high,
Even when Uncle Fred tries to fly.

Love's Melody Through the Chiming Bells

Jingle bells ringing, we croon off the tune,
Off-key on the chorus, we sing to the moon.
Dancing in pajamas, oh what a parade,
Our love is the music we joyfully made.

The cookies are gone, and so is the pie,
But no one is worried; we'll give it a try.
With joy in our hearts and our giggles all swell,
It's love that surrounds us, oh can't you just tell?

Serendipity in the Air of Togetherness

Snowflakes are falling, and so is the cake,
Oh dear, it's a riot, but look at theake!
We snuggle and shuffle, in shadows we play,
Finding our laughter in the cold of the day.

As we toast with our drinks, and toast that same bread,
Who put mustard in eggnog? We're both seeing red!
But it's all in good jest, our hearts all aglow,
In this warmth of togetherness, love steals the show.

Evergreen Hugs

In a forest dressed in white,
Even trees dance with delight.
Squirrels in hats, what a sight,
As snowflakes tumble, oh so light.

Jingle bells on every branch,
Raccoons join in with their prance.
All are merry, in a trance,
Spreading joy, with a joyful chance.

Frogs in coats sing their tunes,
While owls hoot under bright moons.
Laughter echoes among cartooned,
As nature hums its festive swoons.

With ribbons wrapped around the pines,
Each hug from branches feels divine.
Nature giggles, so interlined,
In this merry tale of twines.

Laughter in the Air

A merry tune starts to play,
With giggles bouncing every way.
In cozy homes, where kids will sway,
Laughter spills like drink on a tray.

Cats in stockings, dogs in bows,
Children chase snowflakes, striking poses.
Grandpa's jokes, as funny as prose,
The laughter grows, and still it flows.

Hot cocoa chugged, a sugary race,
Fingers sticky, oh, what a case!
Chubby cheeks in a playful embrace,
As joy sparkles and fills the space.

Muffins dropped, they giggle and share,
Snowball fights start that don't require care.
With each laugh, love's in thick air,
These moments are magic, rare beyond compare.

Mistletoe Moments

Underneath the sticky green,
Awkward hugs cause quite a scene.
Uncle Joe slips, loses his lean,
While Aunt Sue dances like a queen.

Kisses stolen with parties in tow,
Child giggles at all that they know.
Boys blushing, oh, what a show,
Finding hearts beneath the glow.

With fruity punch that stains the floor,
Everyone's swaying, laughing for more.
A hidden cat jumps through the door,
Catching kisses, oh, what's in store?

So here's to moments, mistletoe neat,
Where love comes wrapped as a treat.
In the chaos, it's nothing but sweet,
With laughter, it just can't be beat!

The Gift of Presence

Unwrap the laughter like a song,
The best gift is where we belong.
Time spent together, right or wrong,
In our heart, each laugh is strong.

Gifts piled high, but none compare,
To moments shared, so full of flair.
With family gathered, joy's in the air,
As we trade giggles and playful stares.

Grandma's cookies, slightly burnt,
Uncle's song, with notes that turn.
A shared wink, whereby we learn,
That love's the flame for which we yearn.

So let's raise our cups, let's rejoice,
With every chuckle, here's the choice.
Among the wrapping, we find our voice,
In the gift of presence, we all rejoice!

Tinsel and Tenderness

Tinsel twinkling on the tree,
My cat thinks it's for her glee.
She leaps and bounds with such delight,
Leaving me to guard the lights.

Grandma's cookies, oh so sweet,
Might just cause a sugar feat.
Uncle Joe is stuck in his chair,
With crumbs and frosting in his hair.

Starry Nights and Warm Lights

Starry skies and reindeer dreams,
Inflatable Santa makes me scream.
Neighbors taunt with lights so bright,
I'm tangled in my own string plight.

Hot cocoa spills, what a mess!
Marshmallow snowmen, I confess.
Dad's blue socks, a festive sight,
They glow like stars in the night!

Cherished Memories Revisited

Photos stuck on sticky wall,
Watch us grow, oh what a haul!
Mom's big sweater from the past,
Looks like a cozy baggy cast.

Silly hats we used to wear,
Mom still thinks that they're all fair.
Laughing hard 'til we can't breathe,
These moments are the best reprieve.

The Fireplace of Remembrance

Fireplace crackles, sparks in flight,
Dad says it's really just his might.
Socks on the mantel by mistake,
My favorite ones for goodness' sake!

Siblings gather, tales are spun,
Of holiday pranks and laughter fun.
A dancing jingle, it's quite a show,
Even the pets want in on the glow!

The Spirit of Giving

With socks on the mantel, quite out of place,
A cat steals the turkey, oh what a chase!
Santa trips over a pile of gifts,
While auntie just giggles and lightly sifts.

The reindeer are running, they've lost their way,
One's stuck in the chimney, what a display!
Uncle Bob's snoring, his belly's too full,
As laughter erupts like a big, joyful bull.

Warmth Beneath Frosty Eaves

Frosty the snowman won't stop doing flips,
While hot cocoa spills and the kettle tips.
Dancing with cookies, a powdered delight,
Rudolph's got moves, oh what a sight!

Under the mistletoe, we all take our stance,
But Cousin Louisa just can't find her pants!
With marshmallow snowballs, a sweet little fight,
This holiday frolic makes everything bright.

Firelight Whispers

Crackling wood and shadows look like a show,
The dog's in the stocking, what a cute grow!
We're wrapped in our blankets, snug and secure,
But grandma's snoring, it's hard to endure!

The firelight dances and flickers about,
But Timmy's caught wishing his robots would sprout.
With jingling laughter, the night carries on,
As bedtime approaches, we're barely drawn!

Joy Wrapped in Red and Green

Presents piled high, yet chaos ensues,
With Dad dressed as Santa, all stuck in his shoes!
Sister's serenading, the dog starts to howl,
As we all join in with a holiday growl!

Tinsel's in tangles, the tree's gone askew,
While Uncle Pete's searching for a shiny shoe.
Gifts made with laughter, each one has a twist,
In the heart of the season, there's so much to miss!

Traces of Love in Sugar and Spice

Cookies in the oven make us cheer,
The cat just swiped them, oh dear, oh dear!
Flour on our faces, icing in our hair,
Laughter fills the kitchen as we dance without a care.

Sugar plums twinkle, sprinkles fly,
Dad slipped on frosting, oh my, oh my!
We're baking with glee, but it's chaos, no doubt,
Yet these sweet little moments, we'll never live without.

Embracing the Mirth of Giving

Tangled lights and a tree that won't stand,
Unwrapping the gifts, there's chaos at hand.
Grandma's knitted socks, too big for my feet,
Each one's a treasure, though they're hard to beat.

We laugh at the paper, it flies like a kite,
The dog's in the ribbons, oh what a sight!
Giggles erupt as the wrapping we tear,
For joy is the gift that we happily share.

Beneath the Evergreen's Tender Boughs

Underneath the branches, we whisper and scheme,
Fighting for space, just like in a dream.
The ornaments jingle, the lights start to blink,
Timing our laughter to the eggnog drink.

The tree's a bit crooked, it sways in the breeze,
And there's Uncle Joe, who won't stop with the cheese!
We gather together with stories to tell,
In this wild winter wonder, we're casting a spell.

Frosted Windows and Love's Reflection

Outside the snow falls, it's chilly like ice,
Inside we're warm, and everything's nice.
Hot cocoa in hand, with marshmallows afloat,
But Dad spilled his drink, oh what a funny boat!

The windows frost over, our breath forms a cloud,
Singing off-key, we're all feeling proud.
With shadows that dance, and laughter that glows,
This is how magic and silliness flows.

Radiant Joy in Every Corner

In the kitchen, cookies burn,
Dad wears a Santa hat with stern.
Someone's stirring punch too hot,
Mum's tracking down the dog we forgot.

The lights blink like they're in a race,
Uncle Fred's shoes are out of place.
Laughter echoes, gifts in a pile,
Grandpa's snoring, but that's his style.

A cat climbs high on the tree,
Knocking baubles joyfully.
Cousins chase under mistletoe,
The holiday spirit steals the show.

Socks on heads, we dance with glee,
Even the goldfish joins this spree.
Each giggle wrapped in sheer delight,
Together, everything feels just right.

The Embrace of Togetherness

Gathered 'round with faces bright,
Uncle Joe sings off-key tonight.
A toast with soda, cheers in the air,
Sister's wig, quite a wild affair.

Mom's dessert falls, but who's to fret?
Dad grabs it fast like a safety net.
We dress the dog in an ugly sweater,
Even he looks like he feels better!

Sharing secrets, tales all mixed,
Grandma's knitting – another fix!
Mismatched socks piled on the floor,
Chaos reigns, but who could ask more?

Carols sung while we dance goofy,
A holiday party never gets moody.
Wrapped in laughter, warm and tight,
Togetherness shines through the night.

Bell's Ringing with Cheer

Bells ringing loud, what a delight,
Cousins jump around, what a sight!
Presents stacked, but watch your step,
Who knew wrapping could cause such prep?

Jingle socks on special feet,
Dancing in sync, a funny beat.
Mom yells "Dinner!" – we all sprint,
Dad's surprise? More glitter, no hint!

Snowflakes swirl in a wacky storm,
Man's best friend is now the warm.
All the chaos, oh what a game,
Each silly mishap, not quite the same!

Jokes exchanged 'til cheeks are red,
On this night, who needs a bed?
To laughter's tune we raise our cheer,
The joy of the season, loud and clear.

Above the Silent Night

Above the silent night so bright,
Someone's carols, quite the fright.
Out in the snow, we make a mess,
Sledding down, hope no one's stressed!

Tinsel tangled in every nook,
Dad's schedule looks like an open book.
Snowmen giggle, hats all askew,
Kids toss snowballs; one just flew!

Cocoa spills, but we just grin,
Puppy's paws leave a path within.
A family photo with silly poses,
Laughter and joy, that's how it goes!

Later that night, with rest in sight,
We hug so tight, it feels just right.
Memories made, like stars shine bright,
Above us all, love takes flight.

Snowflakes of Affection

Snowflakes dance and twirl about,
Landing softly, causing a shout!
Innocent laughter, kids in a pile,
Fighting snowballs, with a cheeky smile.

Hot cocoa spills and mugs collide,
Everyone's laughter, oh, what a ride!
Marshmallows flying, it's a grand mess,
Sledding to glory, who'd guess, no stress?

Furry mittens and socks askew,
Slip on the ice, who knew it grew?
Giggles echo under the stars,
Snow angels made, our very own cars.

As snowflakes fall, it's a wacky scene,
Joy in the chaos, oh, how it serene!
Let's map out our fun, with a wink and cheer,
In this frosty playground, there's nothing to fear!

Candlelit Dreams

A flicker here, a shadow there,
The cat's in the tree, oh, beyond repair!
Candlelight wobbles, brings giggles with fright,
While Aunt Edna's knitting, oh, what a sight!

Cookies piled high on a wobbly dish,
Each one a promise, each bite a wish.
Sugar plums dance around the room,
While uncles start snoring, spreading their gloom.

Whispers of stories from long, long ago,
As kids roll their eyes and peek at the glow.
Grandpa's tall tales, all utterly wild,
Makes every heart smile, even the mild.

With laughter and crumbs making quite the scene,
Candlelit dreams keep the evening keen.
We snicker and chuckle as the tales unfold,
In this cozy chaos, life's treasures are gold!

Sledding Down Memory Lane

Decked out in gear that's far too tight,
Sledding begins, oh, what a sight!
Hats fall off and scarves unwind,
Wobbling down slopes, every turn is blind.

The thrill of the ride, cheers fill the air,
Watch out for trees, and dodge that bear!
Down we go, with shrieks and flails,
A conga line of friends, let's follow the trails!

Snowballs fly, a friendly upset,
Wet cheeks and laughs, no hint of regret.
Up the hill, we trudge with glee,
Only to tumble, oh, just wait and see!

With cocoa in hand and tales in our hearts,
Sledding down memories is where it all starts.
Laughter and joy in the winter's embrace,
Creating our story, finding our place!

The Season of Togetherness

Gather around for a bumpy ride,
With Uncle Joe driving, who needs pride?
The tree's decorated with quirky old flair,
And Grandma insists on pearls in our hair!

Tinsel and laughter, twinkling bright,
As socks hang low, goodwill takes flight.
Burnt cookies bubble, what a strange delight,
While kids steal bites, oh, what a sight!

Silly games lead to raucous fun,
Mom tries her best, but can't outrun!
A dance party starts, with moves of the past,
Spinning and twirling, making it last.

So here's to the love in our funny ways,
In the season we cherish, we sing songs of praise.
With laughter and cheer, and hearts open wide,
Together we celebrate, side by side!

Enveloped in Love and Light

Under the tree, a cat lays down,
With bows in his hair, he wears a crown.
Tinsel flies like a wild kite,
As kids giggle at the silly sight.

Gifts wrapped tight, all in a heap,
Watch out for Grandma, she's losing sleep!
She's baking cookies, but here's the twist,
She added salt, so it's hard to resist!

The laughter rolls like snowballs neat,
But watch your toes, 'cause here comes the fleet.
Siblings throwing gifts, a merry scuffle,
Presents unwrapped, but so is the shuffle.

Yet amid the chaos, love does shine,
As hearts collide over mugs of wine.
Raise a cheer, it's time to unwind,
In this funny mess, the best you'll find!

Stars in the Frost

The lights twinkle like stars on the ground,
And Dad's dance moves are wildly renowned.
In a sweater that's two sizes too small,
He spins and stumbles, we can only guffaw.

Snowmen with noses made of fresh carrots,
And one with a wig, like a celebrity's merits.
But wait, what's that? A snowball in flight!
Right in the face of a man with a fright!

Jingle bells ringing, but slightly out of tune,
Sister sings loudly, like a howling raccoon.
With cookies that might just break a tooth,
It's a wacky ride, but we love the truth.

Under the mistletoe, awkwardness sparks,
As a dad gives a wink in the merriest parks.
We laugh 'til we cry, oh what a delight,
Stars in our eyes, this joy feels just right!

Ambers of Fondness

The fireplace crackles, a warm little glow,
While Aunt Edna's knitting brings laughter and woe.
A sweater for Fido, three sizes too wide,
We're laughing so hard, Fido's got pride!

The eggnog flows like a sweet little stream,
But Dad's got a secret—whipped cream's the dream!
It lands on his nose, like a frosty delight,
We can't stop our giggles, it's pure festive light.

With cookies that crumble and cocoa so sweet,
Cousins are pranking, oh what a treat!
The lights are all tangled, what a great sight,
It's a festival of fun, with pure joy in flight!

So here's to the moments, both silly and grand,
Ambers of fondness we'll always expand.
Through laughter and love, we gather each year,
In these crazy times, all our hearts feel near.

Embracing the Season's Glow

The snowflakes flutter, like butterflies' dance,
While Uncle Joe tries his luck at romance.
He's dressed up as Santa, with beard askew,
His charm's undeniable, much to our view!

Cookies that sparkle with glitter and sprinkles,
In the chaos of frosting, the laughter just crinkles.
A gingerbread house that leans like the Tower,
We cheer it along, giving it power.

Kids on a sugar rush zooming around,
They trip on the garland all over the ground.
We dodge little feet in this comical maze,
Wrapped up in joy, in a merry haze.

Through all the blunders, we find our way back,
With hugs and warm hearts in this festive flack.
So here's to the bliss that makes spirits glow,
In this funny season, let laughter sew!

Kindness Drifting Like Snowflakes

On frosty nights, we roast our toes,
While sneaky socks slide and all else goes.
With cocoa spills and giggles so bright,
We share warm hugs to chase off the bite.

Laughter echoes with each snowball thrown,
As chickens dance in the yard, well-known.
The cat won't budge, he'll just stay inside,
While we all tumble down the icy slide.

The tree's all twinkly, with ornaments askew,
A pickle lurking, oh what will we do?
Peppermint myrrh and a sprinkle of fun,
Our silly hearts dance with joy on the run.

So let's raise a cheer, with joy on our face,
And don those reindeer ears for the race.
With laughter as light as the falling snow,
Let kindness drift, let the love overflow!

Heartstrings Woven in Holiday Harmony

In our cozy nook, we sing off-key,
While Uncle Fred brings his famous tea.
The cookies burn, the dog snags a bite,
Yet we laugh with glee, it's a wondrous sight.

We've tangled lights like spaghetti in cheer,
And grandma's stories, oh, we lend an ear.
With mismatched socks and a gust of cheer,
We're the jolliest crew, full of good cheer.

In the midst of chaos, a snowman stands tall,
While cheeky elves find gifts for us all.
Frosty beat-boxing in the yard just now,
Our heartstrings twine tight, just look at us, wow!

So let's toast with cider, with mugs raised high,
As we tell silly jokes that make spirits fly.
With hugs all around, in sweet harmony,
Love's music plays on, eternally free.

Winter's Embrace

Bundled up tight, we troop through the snow,
With scarves wrapped so snug, our faces aglow.
The hot chocolate spills, oops! But look at the fun,
As whipped cream battles are joyfully won!

Snowflakes swirl down like confetti from the sky,
While grandpa does silly dances, oh my!
The dog's got a hat, but he thinks it's a toy,
We giggle and laugh; oh, what a joy!

In the blink of an eye, cookies disappear,
We'll blame it on elves, but we know it's sheer.
Socks on the ceiling, it's quite a bizarre
But our hearts are aglow—yes, that's who we are!

Warmed by the glow of the firelight dance,
With hearts intertwining, we take a chance.
So here's to the joy that winter extends,
In this season of laughter, where love never ends!

Twinkling Hearts Under Starry Skies

Under a blanket of shimmering light,
We chase after fireflies, oh what a sight!
The stars are giggling, they wink and they sway,
As we roast marshmallows the silly way.

With snowmen donning their carrot red noses,
We wear silly hats, yes, that's how it goes.
Grandma's recipe's a twist of delight,
And the taste of our laughter, oh, it's out of sight!

Bubbles in the punch make a fizzy parade,
With dancing and singing, our worries all fade.
In twinkling moments, our hearts leap and glide,
In this wintery wonder, we all take pride.

So gather around, join the merry old tune,
With joy in our hearts, let's dance by the moon.
For under these stars, where the magic ignites,
It's love we find here, in our starry nights!

Sledding Through Heartfelt Joy

The snowflakes dance, oh what a sight,
We sled down hills, hearts so light.
With cocoa spills and laughter loud,
We make a mess, we're oh-so-proud.

Our noses red, we giggle and cheer,
As snowballs fly, the truth is clear.
Together we stumble, together we glide,
In the heart's winter wonder, we take a ride.

The dogs keep chasing, the kids make a fuss,
Who knew sledding could be this much plus?
With cheeks like cherries, we raise a toast,
To winter's folly, the one we love the most!

As twilight sets, we gather round,
With tales of mishaps, laughter profound.
In snowman gear, we pose so brave,
Sledding through joy, our hearts we save.

Warmth of an Unspoken Bond

The light's so dim, the glow so bright,
We share a glance, all feels just right.
With gifts all wrapped, and secrets stored,
We sip on cheer, our hearts adored.

In comfy socks, we dance around,
As Aunt Edna's fruitcake hits the ground.
A nudge, a wink, the laughter flows,
Together we glow, like mistletoe bows.

The jokes we spin, the fun we wield,
An unspoken bond, our love revealed.
In the cozy chaos, we find our place,
Warmth in the giggles, a sweet embrace.

With every chuckle, another surprise,
As we feast upon all our favorite pies.
In this wild mess, we feel so free,
Unraveled together, in blissful spree.

The Magic of Generosity

The bells are ringing, the carols sing,
Generosity's here, let the joy take wing.
With awkward gifts and misfit bows,
We share the warmth, as good will grows.

A cactus wrapped in bright red cheer,
For Uncle Jim, oh the laughter near.
The sweaters clash, the colors scream,
In this merry madness, we chase a dream.

With cookies traded, and stories shared,
Each tiny gift, made with love, declared.
For who needs norms when smiles abound?
In the magic of giving, pure joy is found.

A neighbor's fruitcake, a token from us,
Though it's rock-hard, it's done with fuss.
Together we giggle, that's how it goes,
In the spirit of sharing, everyone grows.

Hope Wrapped in Ribbon

A box of wonders, ribbons all bright,
Inside are dreams, wrapped up tight.
We giggle and snicker as we shake and peek,
What's in this treasure? It's a fun little tweak!

The mischief unfolds, as we tear away,
With gifts of giggles that brighten the day.
Each paper crinkle sings out loud,
In the hope of joy, we feel so proud.

Uncles in elf hats, a sight to behold,
As we unwrap laughter, our hearts turn gold.
With silly surprises, the fun won't stop,
It's mingling magic, we're ready to swap!

From candy canes to socks with flair,
In this jolly chaos, we all share.
A hope wrapped in laughter, a ribbon of cheer,
In this joyful season, friends and family near.

Starlit Gatherings

Under twinkling lights we meet,
With socks so bright, not quite a feat.
Laughter bubbles like warm stew,
Who stepped on whose foot? Oh, is that you?

Mittens tangled in a rush,
Cat's in the tree, oh what a hush!
We toast with mugs that spill a bit,
Cheers to the falls, and mishaps we'll commit!

The prince and princess silly dance,
Two left feet, a clumsy chance.
Grab your partner, spin around,
Oops! The punch is now on the ground!

In this jolly, goofy spree,
Love serves up a cup of glee.
With hugs so tight and hearts so bright,
Together we sparkle, what a sight!

Chiming Joy

Bells are ringing in the cheer,
Yet Auntie's gift brings out a sneer.
Is that a fruitcake or a doorstop?
We'll laugh and eat till we all drop!

Singing carols in high-pitch,
Grandpa joins in, what a switch!
He starts to dance, what a scene,
Oh dear, thank goodness for the floor routine!

The cookies look a bit askew,
Gingerbread men, do they have two?
With icing on our noses bright,
We munch and giggle through the night.

In every note, a spark of fun,
With family, this race is won.
So grab a laugh, and join the tune,
We'll send this joy to the moon!

A Symphony of Kindness

Plucking strings with playful flair,
But someone's off-key — is it Bear?
He howls a note that's truly wild,
We all erupt, it's so beguiled!

Echoes fill the kitchen space,
With pots and pans, we're in a race.
Stirring soup that's lumpy still,
With ten big spoons, we miss the will!

Handmade gifts with glitter glue,
A hat for Dad that is quite askew.
He wears it proud, though it's a sight,
As laughter lifts us, oh what a night!

In every act of silly grace,
We find the love in each embrace.
Together we sing, shout, and cheer,
In this crazy fun, we hold dear!

Homemade Cookies and Shared Smiles

Rolling dough, a wondrous mess,
Flour fights, now who would guess?
Sprinkles flying like confetti,
Here comes the cat, oh, what a petty!

Choc'late chips in goofy style,
Each cookie baked has its own smile.
Burnt on the edge, still tastes divine,
Guess we'll just call it charred wine!

With milk that spills, or does it flow?
A ghost story told, oh no, oh no!
Except it's Grandma, missed the plot,
Now we all laugh, she's really hot!

The best recipe? That's simple, friend,
It's love, laughter, that won't end.
So we bake, share, and in between,
We make the sweetest, funnest scene!

Whispers of Warmth in Winter's Embrace

Snowflakes dance with glee,
As hot cocoa spills on me.
The cat chases ribbons, oh so wild,
While Grandma tells tales, but they're reviled.

Mittens mismatched, a sight to behold,
Dad's slapstick moves, never gets old.
We fumble and trip on the icy street,
Laughing until we can't find our feet.

Lights twinkle bright, a comical sight,
Uncle Fred's tree leans a tad to the right.
Eggnog spills on Aunt Ruth's new dress,
And yet we would never love it less.

Through laughter and joy, we all convene,
Sharing our dreams, like a comical scene.
In winter's embrace, we find our cheer,
Together with love, we hold each dear.

Twinkling Stars and Heartfelt Wishes

Under a sky where the stars play tag,
My wishes are strong, they never lag.
But a squirrel steals my cookie stash,
Now holiday peace has turned into a clash.

With reindeer prancing on the roof,
Dad whispers loud about his goof.
He believes Santa's real cool and slick,
But we know he's just a funny old trick.

Decorating trees with clumsy finesse,
A toadstool on top? We call it progress.
Laughing so hard, we start to snort,
Family love and laughter, our jolly sport.

As we share stories and pass the pie,
Outcomes hilariously funny, oh my!
Twinkling stars above, while we're below,
In tender moments, our hearts in tow.

The Hearth's Glow Beneath the Mistletoe

By the fire we gather, tales spinning round,
Who's the biggest jokester? Oh, it's so profound!
Aromas of pies mixed with playful jeers,
Tickling the fancy as laughter appears.

Grandpa's old jokes might give you the shivers,
But don't tell him that; he might just have quivers.
The mistletoe hangs, though it's slightly askew,
We steal awkward kisses, oh, just a few!

The puppy runs wild with chaos in tow,
Chasing socks and slippers, don't ask how it knows.
Fireside stories bring chuckles and cheer,
As our quirky love story grows year after year.

With mischief and mirth and a sprinkle of glee,
We craft memories, truly wild and free.
In the hearth's glow, joy is our decree,
Bonding together, just you wait and see!

Together in the Softest Snowfall

In the fluff of white, we tumble and roll,
Snowmen with noses made out of coal.
Giggles erupt with each snowy plop,
As we build castles, we never will stop.

Sledding down hills in mismatched attire,
Collecting cold snow like a winter lyre.
Dad's pants split wide on a daring ride,
And all we can do is laugh and divide.

Snowball fights with stealth and grace,
But the dog joins in, what a wild chase!
Landing in snow with a puff and a thud,
What once was a game now resembles a flood.

Here's to the warmth beneath icy skies,
With laughter as bright as the northern lights' rise.
In snowflakes and smiles, our love trumps all,
Together, forever, we're bound by the snowfall.

Hearts Entwined by Candlelight

In the glow of lights so bright,
We dance around this festive sight.
Grandma's cookies, oh what a tease,
Half are missing—where's the cheese?

Uncle Joe sings off-key, my dear,
His version of jingle bells, oh sheer!
With every note, we fall to the floor,
Laughing so hard, we can't take more.

Kids are hiding behind the tree,
Whispering secrets, feeling so free.
Gift wrap battles are in full swing,
Tape sticks everywhere, oh what a thing!

At night we share tales, quite absurd,
Like the one of the bird that lost its herd.
Laughter erupts, echoing the night,
Hearts entwined, all feeling just right.

Sweet Laughter on Frosty Nights

Snowflakes twirl in the chilly air,
Hot cocoa spills, oh, what a scare!
With marshmallows flying, we cheer and play,
Who knew winter games could go this way?

A snowman's hat, oh dear, it's gone,
One puppy snatched it, now he's the don.
We chase him 'round, slipping and sliding,
Laughter echoes, joy unapologetically gliding.

As stockings hang upon the wall,
You bet we'll fill them—wobbling thrall!
A rubber chicken? Why not, you bet!
Gifts of giggles, we'll never forget!

We pile on blankets, warm and snug,
With stories of elves who liked to chug.
Under the twinkle of lights so bright,
Sweet laughter echoes through the frosty night.

The Magic of Kindness Wrapped in Red

With candy canes, we spread good cheer,
Our neighbors' lights are blinding, dear!
We sneak a peek at their bright display,
Laughing as we munch on sweets, hooray!

Cookies delivered with a wink and a smile,
Everyone knows it's been quite a while.
Whiskers on kittens, oh what a sight,
Magic of kindness ignites the night.

The reindeer games in the front yard unfold,
Uncle's the judge, quite a sight to behold!
"We're flying!" they shout, but land on a cat,
Oh, the mayhem of laughter; where are we at?

With ribbons and bows, we wrap up the fun,
Tangled in lights, and oh, a pun!
In this chaos, we find our thread,
A spirit of kindness all wrapped in red.

Sipping Joy by a Tumbling Fire

Near the flames, we gather tight,
Sipping honeysuckle tea, what a delight!
Grandpa spills tales of his youth,
While little ones giggle, missing the truth.

The log does crackle, sparks do fly,
As we roast marshmallows, oh me, oh my!
S'mores turn into blobs, a sticky mess,
Each bite brings laughter, we must confess.

A cat jumps up, thinks he's the king,
Pawing at treat bags, oh what a thing!
We swat at him gently, with giggles and sighs,
Wishing on stars in the cold winter skies.

As night embraces the world outside,
We stay in our circle, hearts open wide.
With joy in our cups and warmth from the fire,
We drink to the moments that never tire.

A Tapestry of Togetherness and Cheer

In mismatched socks we dance and twirl,
With pies that wobble, and ribbons that swirl.
Uncle Joe's joke that makes no sense,
Has us laughing 'til we feel immense!

We wrap our gifts in newspaper flair,
The dog joins in with a mischievous stare.
Grandma's knitting, oh what a sight,
A scarf for the cat, it's quite the fright!

Caught under mistletoe, we play our part,
With cheeky smiles and a wink of the heart.
The tree leans sideways, surely it knows,
Who's been sneaking all the candy canes' prose!

Laughter echoes as we hear a loud thud,
When Dad slipped on the floor, oh the love in the mudd!
With full plates and hearts, cherish the cheer,
In this bright tapestry, love draws us near.

Joyful Voices Carried on the Wind

Singing loudly, off-key in the cold,
We belt out tunes, both silly and bold.
Neighbors peek out, with a puzzled grin,
As Aunt Sally spins in a turkey skin!

The kids giggle loud, with cookies to share,
Sprinkling flour, they float like air.
Muffins explode and frosting must fly,
As laughter erupts like stars in the sky!

Roasting marshmallows, the sticks start to bend,
Who knew hot chocolate could break, just pretend?
With whipped cream beards and hats piled high,
We melt in joy as the night races by!

The tales we tell, wrapped in giggle and poke,
Breathe life into moments, like a warm, funny cloak.
Voices merge with the winds, wild and free,
In joyful rhythms, it's pure jubilee!

Radiance Found in Handwritten Wishes

With crumpled letters and ink that's run,
We scribble our dreams, oh what fun!
A wish for socks, or a cat that sings,
Handwritten joy, oh the laughter it brings!

Ribbon chaos and paper cuts galore,
Decorating carefully, yet more is a chore.
The lights twinkle, competing for show,
As Aunt Edna's headwear starts to glow!

Cards once so serious, now make no sense,
With doodles and jokes that tickle our defense.
We gather around, share the silly and sweet,
Reciting our wishes, like a grand little treat!

In every scribble, a sparkle or twink,
Radiant moments tug at our link.
With joy overflowing, we cherish this spree,
Handwritten wishes bring us glee.

Gathering Under the Ruby Sky

Under a sky that sparks ruby bright,
We gather close, sharing warmth and delight.
With snowflakes dancing, oh what a view,
While Grandpa insists he's still a cool dude!

Hot cocoa spills, and giggles resound,
As snowmen assemble, they tumble and bound.
With carrot noses that somehow have flopped,
And brotherly pranks that just can't be stopped!

The fire crackles, sharing tales bold,
As we sway like marshmallows, all sugary and gold.
With each silly joke that brings forth a snort,
Our hearts beat as one, in this mashed-up report!

Beneath the amenities, bonds are renewed,
Festivities woven, and laughter ensued.
Gathered together, we're all one big crew,
Under the ruby sky, love shines right through!

Frosted Memories

Rudolph went to the gym, so spry,
But insisted he could still fly.
Santa yelled, 'Oh dear, take a seat!',
While munching on cookies, oh what a treat!

The snowman danced with a wiggle so grand,
While gales of laughter spread through the land.
Hot cocoa spilled as friends had a ball,
With marshmallows bouncing and missing the wall!

The elves tried baking a pie, oh what fun,
It turned into soup, and then on the run.
With sugar and spice, and everything nice,
They laughed at their mess, not once thinking twice!

Under the mistletoe, they started a race,
With candy cane prizes, they all found their pace.
Together they cheered, snowflakes dancing like pros,
Creating sweet memories, wrapped up in bows.

Unity Beneath the Snow

A squirrel stole Santa's hat for a nest,
While the reindeer giggled, simply the best.
The jingle bells jingled, a cacophony loud,
As folks made snow angels, all cheerful and proud.

Pinecones turned to ornaments, who'd have guessed?
Adorned with glitter and squirrelly zest.
They cheered as they decorated the tree,
With popcorn chains from a wild jubilee!

Mittens mismatched, a sight to behold,
As the winter winds whispered tales of the bold.
Together they laughed, what a comical sight,
Around in circles, all jolly and bright!

Underneath snowflakes, friendships took flight,
With snowball confetti, they danced through the night.
Building a spirit that couldn't be quelled,
In unity's warm hug, they all felt compelled.

Hearts Entwined in the Chill

The penguins decided to throw a grand ball,
With chicken dance music, they'd welcome it all.
A walrus donned goggles, a fluffy pink coat,
Snowflakes were swirling, oh what a quote!

The sleigh got stuck in a mound of deep snow,
While the kids cheered, 'Come on, we won't let it go!'
With laughter so hearty, they gave it a shove,
A slide down the hill is what they all love!

Frostbite forgot, as they played hide-and-seek,
The laughter echoing, at times it was squeak!
Hearts twinkled brightly, more than starry lights,
Wrapped in joy, on those magical nights.

They shared all their stories with whimsical flair,
From mischief to giggles, to true love laid bare.
In the chill of the night, friendships ignited,
With each goofy moment, their spirits delighted!

A Tapestry of Togetherness

The cat had a dance with the Christmas tree,
While the dog just barked, 'Come look at me!'
Ornaments scattered, a spectacle grand,
As chaos ensued, oh, isn't it grand?

Jingle bells jingled in sync with the fun,
As kids made a wish on the bright golden sun.
In wrapping paper wars, they'd dive and they'd roll,
With laughter contagious, they filled up the hole!

Hot chocolate rivers ran through the cheer,
Mugs overflowing while slipping on gear.
The laughter echoed 'til the end of the day,
With joy overflowing, in each silly play!

Family together with hearts full of glee,
Spreading the warmth of sweet memories.
Under the glow of the lights up above,
They spun through the night, wrapped up in love!

A Journey Home by Lantern Light

With lanterns glowing, we roam the street,
  Caroling elves, dancing on their feet.
  The snowmen giggle, noses in a row,
  As we trip on laughter, down they go!

The sleigh bells jingle, a cat on the roof,
Uncle Joe's snoring, still brings us the proof.
  We gather for mischief, what a delight,
  It's hard to be quiet on this festive night.

Grandma's baking cookies, oh what a treat,
But we sneak the dough, can't resist the sweet.
With flour on noses, we're merry and bright,
  Our home is a circus, such a funny sight!

We swap silly gifts, all wrapped up with care,
  A pink woolly sweater, who would dare?
Yet each hug we share, both warm and sincere,
Makes the journey home loud with holiday cheer!

Silent Nights and Shared Dreams

Whispers of frosty air, quiet as can be,
We dream up a snowman named 'Wobbly'.
Cocoa spills over while we giggle and snort,
As mittens wrestle on the warmest report.

The stars above shimmer, twinkling with glee,
We spy on the reindeer, it's hard to agree.
When cookies go missing, blame the family pet,
His guilty look tells us we've made quite a bet!

With pillows like clouds, we plot dreams for all,
Flying through rooftops, no worries, no fall.
Yet the clock strikes midnight, we're not done,
A pillow fight erupts just for fun!

When morning arrives, oh, what a surprise!
While sleep in our eyes, we're quick to arise.
The laughter is loud, through the tiny old house,
We dance like the elves, and bounce like a mouse!

The Embrace of Familiar Faces

Gathered round the table, a feast to behold,
Uncle Bob's telling tales that are way too old.
Auntie's fruitcake, oh my, what a sight,
It bounces off walls and takes off in flight!

Every grin and chuckle, a story to tell,
As we share our odd dreams, it's hard to excel.
The hugs are as tight as the slacks after lunch,
With playful nudges, we form a big bunch!

Our piles of presents are wonky and weird,
But laughter erupts, this warmth we all cheered.
Right next to the tree, a surprise pops out,
Cousin Fred in a tutu, dancing about!

Sipping on cider, the joy's overflowing,
Each wink and a smile ensures love's a-growing.
With faces so dear, and hearts open wide,
We play out the night like a fun rollercoaster ride!

Threads of Connection in Winter's Quilt

Under the quilt, all snug and tight,
We weave silly stories into the night.
The frost on the windows paints a frosty show,
While giggles and whispers move to and fro.

With treats on the table and games in our hearts,
We craft a wild snowball fight in the arts.
But oh my, the snow, it's packed down so right,
Grandma's got a launchpad, oh what a sight!

Each thread that we stitch is with laughter and care,
The mittens and hats that we're eager to wear.
As the moon bathes the room in a silvery light,
We cherish these moments, holding them tight.

With love boxed up tight, each hug that we share,
Dances through winter, hangs soft in the air.
The gifts may be silly, the joys never fade,
For in our warm hearts, our quilt has been made!

Beneath the Boughs of Joy

The tree wore tinsel like a crown,
As silly kids danced all around.
The cat thought it was meant to climb,
And got stuck there for quite some time.

The cookies vanished, oh what a fright!
The dog was giggling, the thief in the night.
We all laughed hard at the puppy's big grin,
He licked the plate clean, just where to begin!

Grandpa's sweater, a wild display,
With reindeer tumbling in a ballet.
We laughed till we cried, oh what a sight,
As grandma muttered, 'It's hipster tonight!'

So gather ye round, family and friends,
With silly socks and jokes that never end.
Beneath the boughs, we sillily sway,
In our funny hats, we celebrate the day!

A Melody of Warmth and Wonder

The carolers sang, but off-key for sure,
Their harmony sounded like a loud chore.
Yet we joined in, with giggles and glee,
Singing loudly, as off-key as could be.

Hot chocolate spilled down someone's shirt,
A marshmallow battle, oh what a flirt!
With whipped cream mustaches, we took our stand,
A sugary war, all unplanned and unplanned.

Lights twinkled bright, but one strung too low,
A misstep was made, down went the show.
We tangled and jumbled, just like the lights,
But cuddling close turned our woes into delights.

So here's to the moments, the laughter and cheer,
To silly mishaps, and joy that draws near.
In melodies sweet from our hearts we sing,
With warmth and wonder, let the laughter ring!

Love's Frosty Dance

Outside the snowflakes began to swirl,
We bundled up, giving it a whirl.
A snowman stood proudly, carrot nose high,
Until a rogue snowball landed nearby!

We twirled in circles, fell into mounds,
Our giggles echoed, joy knows no bounds.
A penguin slide off the porch hit the run,
Laughter erupted, a slippery fun!

The frostbite grinned, with cheeks all aglow,
While snowball fights came in a fierce flow.
Twirling and stumbling, we danced in the freeze,
Chasing the snowflakes with whimsical ease.

With mittens and laughter, we'll not soon forget,
The moments of joy, they could not upset.
In love's frosty dance, we move to the beat,
With snowflakes and chuckles, life feels so sweet!

Sparkling Moments of Bliss

The glitter and glam on our hands so bright,
We decorated cookies with sheer delight.
Until the dog jumped, oh what a spree,
He stole them all, not leaving one for me!

Then lights popped out, a sight to chunkle,
Our tree went dark, oh what a rumble.
But Grandma's laugh lit the room like a star,
With jokes on repeat, we giggled bizarre.

The wrapping paper was pet confetti,
As paw prints decorated the gifts so ready.
In a mix-up of chaos, we still felt the cheer,
With heartfelt moments, it's the best time of year!

So let's raise a glass, though it's filled with cheer,
To mishaps and giggles that bring us all here.
In sparkling moments, our hearts are aglow,
Let's keep laughing forever, let the fun flow!

Glowing Together

The lights are twinkling, oh what a sight,
We trip on each other, a comical delight.
With tangled garlands, we laugh and we cheer,
Stuck in the tree? Just another new year!

The cookies are baking, the cat's on the floor,
She swipes at the ornaments, wanting to score.
Milk's in the stockings, a wild little thought,
But who needs it? We've lost that fancy countertop!

With snowflakes descending, we toss a few balls,
I hit Uncle Joe, who's laughing through halls.
In snowman attire, he slips with a plop,
This festive shenanigan just won't ever stop!

The spirit of joy, is truly the best,
In this crazy chaos, we're put to the test.
But through all the laughter and festive display,
We glow together, in our silly ballet.

Sipping Cocoa by Candlelight

We gather 'round mugs, with cocoa so thick,
Marshmallows afloat, like a sweet little trick.
The candles both wobble, they dance to and fro,
But drink too fast, and you'll miss the show!

Oh, Auntie's in baubles, her hair's quite the view,
She swears the grand chair was meant just for two.
But as she sits down, she lets out a squeak,
And the chair gives a groan, resulting in cheek!

We sip all together, each story we share,
Of great family figments, and pasts we all bear.
With laughter erupting, who needs a grand feast?
The joy in our hearts is a marvelous beast!

So raise up your mugs, the laughter runs free,
And maybe by morning, we'll fit 'round the tree.
With cocoa and chaos, our love gives a spark,
By candlelight, we'll light up the dark.

Generosity in Full Bloom

A dollar for dinner? Just grab that lost penny!
We're cooking up chaos, with leftovers aplenty.
Each bite is a gamble, like trivia night,
You never know what you'll get in each bite!

Gifts wrapped in newspaper, oh what a sight,
Bows made of spaghetti, we giggle with glee.
Who needs a store when your pantry's a treasure,
Last week's chili? What a festive measure!

With mugs full of smiles, we share and we trade,
A weird little item, but that's how we've played.
In this generous season, with laughter as glue,
What's mine is now yours, yes, even the stew!

So cherish the moments, the quirky, the fun,
For generosity blooms when we all are as one.
We may not have much, but we'll always have cheer,
In our wild, wacky world, joy will persevere!

Threads of Warmth

With needles and yarn, we all knit away,
Grandma's great plan turns into dismay.
Scarves meant for everyone, but one fits the cat,
She prances all proud, can you picture that?

We huddle together, in sweaters that clash,
Colors so bright, it's a dazzling bash.
A fashion parade of mismatched delight,
We strut through the kitchen, our style is just right!

With hot pies in ovens, we set the stage right,
Then Grandma yells, "Watch for that spark! What a fright!"
The smoke signals rise, we all laugh in haste,
Who knew our feast could go up in a blaze?

Yet through these mishaps, our hearts are still warm,
We share in the laughter and bond in the storm.
In threads made of giggles and stories so bright,
Together we glow in this festive delight!

Glimmers of Affection in the Dark

Twinkling lights on every tree,
They shine like bling for all to see.
Santa's stuck, oh what a sight,
Getting cookies turned to fright!

Elves are napping, snoring loud,
While snowmen wear their carrot crown.
Hot cocoa spills, oh what a mess,
Spreading cheer in every stress.

Wrapping gifts with tape in hand,
And things not going as we planned.
Uncle Joe sings off-key at night,
But his jokes bring such delight!

A cat named Mittens climbs the tree,
And thinks it's all just for her spree.
In this chaos, love will blaze,
In a funny, warm embrace!

Snowy Streets of Kindness

Snowflakes dance like quirky dreams,
While kids throw snowballs at the seams.
Fur coats puffed, like fluffy pies,
With frozen toes and giggling cries.

A puppy runs, with a gift in mouth,
But it's just a sock, headed south!
Mittens found, under our cheer,
The snowman waves, but has no ear!

Mrs. Claus lost in a shop,
Her reindeer making shopping stop.
"Just one more toy!" she exclaims with glee,
But accidental chaos there might be!

Laughter bursts from every door,
As neighbors share, who could ask for more?
In these streets, where joy is bright,
Kindness dances in the night!

Holiday Hearts

Gathered 'round the table spread,
With a turkey ready to be fed.
Grandpa sneezes, and pies take flight,
While laughter echoes through the night.

A chair that wobbles, a giddy scream,
The tablecloth conceals a dream.
Everyone fights for the last bite,
Turkey dancing in sheer delight!

Children giggling, hiding presents,
"Oh no!" a cat joins in the essence.
Tinsel tangled, oh what a sight,
Holiday hearts shining so bright!

Fudge and cookies, a messy crew,
Stealing goodies? Oh how they grew!
In moments silly, love does gleam,
In this joyful, festive theme!

The Dance of Togetherness

Neighbors joined for a festive show,
With every twirl, they steal the glow.
A grandpa slips, but takes a bow,
While joy spills out like milking cows!

Dance floors echo with bumping beats,
As everyone shuffles their funny feets.
A grand finale, but wait, oh dear!
A cat has joined, and all disappear!

Gifts exchanged with coy, sly grins,
Little ones giggle as big folks spin.
With warmth and fun, they sway and sway,
In this dance of love, all hearts play!

Oh dear, Uncle Bob's doing the twist,
With Aunt Sue's ribbon caught in his fist!
Yet through the folly, one thing is clear,
Togetherness shines loud and near!